MINNESOTA

WISCONSIN

MICHIGAN

MAINE

NEW YORK

VT. N.H.

MASS.

CONN. R.I.

N.J.

PENNA.

WA

ILLINOIS

INDIANA OHIO

MARYLAND

DEL.

MISSOURI

W.VA.

KENTUCKY

VIRGINIA

ARKANSAS

TENNESSEE

N.C.

SOUTH CAROLINA

MISSISSIPPI ALABAMA GEORGIA

FLORIDA

LOUISIANA

D1468295

Montana. Custer's Last Stand, 1876.

Nebraska. Homestead Nat'l Monument; first homestead under 1862 law.

New Hampshire. Daniel Webster's birthplace, Franklin.

New Mexico. Indian pueblo, Taos.

New Jersey. Washington Crossing State Park, site of landing, 1776.

New York. The Franklin D. Roosevelt shrine, Hyde Park.

Nevada. Comstock Lode, Virginia City.

North Carolina. Roanoke Island, site of Lost Colony.

North Dakota. Fort Abraham Lincoln State Park; pioneer stockades.

Ohio. Battle of Lake Erie, 1813.

Oklahoma. "Sooners" Land Rush. Murals in State Capitol Building.

Oregon. Fur era monument, Astoria.

Pennsylvania. Independence Hall.

Rhode Island. Roger Williams Park.

South Carolina. Fort Sumter, 1861.

South Dakota. Mount Rushmore.

Tennessee. The Hermitage, home of Andrew Jackson, Nashville.

Texas. The Alamo, San Antonio. State's greatest sorrow, greatest glory.

Utah. Mormon Temple, Salt Lake City.

Vermont. Ethan Allen's Green Mountain Boys; Bennington Monument.

Virginia. Cornwallis' surrender to Washington, Yorktown.

Washington. Marker to Capt. Robert Gray, discoverer of Columbia River.

West Virginia. John Brown's. Fort, Harper's Ferry Raid, 1859.

Wisconsin. Marquette and Joliet discover Mississippi; marker at Portage.

Wyoming. Fort Laramie, once most important stronghold in the West.

THE U.S.A. IN COLOR

THE
USA
IN COLOR

BY THE EDITORS OF

HOLIDAY

Published by The Curtis Publishing Company, Philadelphia

Distributed by Doubleday & Company, Inc., Garden City, N.Y.

Library of Congress Catalog Card Number: 56–5243

Printed in the United States of America

THE U.S.A. IN COLOR

Over the past ten years, HOLIDAY has published color photographs of many of the world's most glamorous places. One country has appeared more often than any other. Naturally, that is our own U.S.A. And in this book we have gathered together in permanent form some of the most representative color pictures of the U.S. that have appeared in the pages of our magazine.

Travel is an old American custom and a good one. Those rugged and admirable souls, our forefathers, traveled to get here, and had barely arrived when they started to push down, up and across until the entire continent was opened and looked upon. Today, we, the American people, own more automobiles, more power boats, more private planes than the rest of the world together. We have more miles of paved roads, more strands of sandy beach, more man- and Nature-made lakes, more acres of national parks than any other country in the world. We've always looked upon distance as a challenge and a mile as something to put behind us.

So in THE U.S.A. IN COLOR we give you your own, your native land — in colors often bold and brilliant, sometimes soft and pastel. We apologize for not including every scene dear to Americans. But we hope this volume will help toward a clearer understanding and appreciation of the rewards travel in the United States offers you; that it will inspire you to take to the road; and that it will serve you as a guide and reference in the pleasant future.

TED PATRICK, *Editor*

CONTENTS

Favorite American Tours

Coast-to-Coast: North

THE "big trip" that every American ought to make at least once in his life is the coast-to-coast auto jaunt, taking in some of the National Parks on the way. On a 3700-mile tour from New York to San Francisco (or vice versa, of course) you can take in the Black Hills, Yellowstone, the Grand Tetons and Yosemite, plus many fascinating cities and towns.

Get off to a fast start via the New Jersey Turnpike to Philadelphia, where you must be sure to see Independence Hall with its Liberty Bell and the brand-new Independence Mall. Continue to historic Valley Forge, and there get onto the Pennsylvania Turnpike, the great, divided highway, without a sharp turn or a steep hill, which will carry you the 327 miles to the Ohio line. Continue on the Ohio Turnpike for 240 miles to the Indiana state line, where you connect with U. S. 20 to Chicago.

In Chicago you ought to allow a few days to see things like the Chicago Natural History Museum and the Shedd Aquarium, to swim from a Lake Michigan beach and to dine in Chicago's wonderful restaurants. Take U. S. 12 out of Chicago, through the lovely, rolling, lake country of Southern Wisconsin, and pause to look over Madison, built between two lakes. Madison is both the state capital and the seat of the University of Wisconsin, which has a particularly beautiful campus. Next stop, the Wisconsin Dells, fantastically scenic rocks carved by the Wisconsin River cutting a 10-mile channel 150 feet deep through sandstone.

From the Wisconsin Dells, follow U. S. 16 a distance of 382 miles to Sioux Falls, South Dakota, a run that takes you across the Mississippi at La Crosse, Wisconsin, and through rolling prairie, farm and dairy country in which wild flowers thrive. From Sioux Falls it is 367 miles to Rapid City, South Dakota, still on U. S. 16, which crosses the Missouri, then cuts through rolling ranch terrain and the weirdly beautiful Badlands to the Black Hills.

In Rapid City see Dinosaur Park, on Skyline Drive, with its lifesize steel and concrete reproductions of prehistoric animals. Then circle south to the old mining town of Keystone where you start the three-mile climb to Mt. Rushmore and its majestically sculptured Presidential heads. Wind through the Telescope Tunnels up to the lookout point on Iron Mountain and continue through Custer State Park to magnificent Sylvan Lake. Head north on U. S. 85 Alt., to the northern Black Hills; visit the picturesque, frontier mining town of Deadwood, and Spearfish where the Black Hills Passion Play is given in summer.

It is 470 miles from Rapid City to Yellowstone National Park, via U. S. 14 and 16 to Buffalo, 16 to Worland, 20 to Greybull, and 14-20 into Yellowstone via Cody, cutting through the Big Horn Mountains between Buffalo and Worland. In July, August or early September, the alternate route, U. S. 14 through Sheridan rather than Buffalo, is worth trying, since it crosses the high, spectacular hump of the Big Horn.

Yellowstone will be worth a good stay. It is a fantastic land of geysers, colorful canyons, glass mountains, great falls, a gigantic mountain lake, shy small animals and not-so-shy bears. Accommodations run from first-class hotels (located at Old Faithful, Canyon, and Mammoth Hot Springs) to cabin colonies and campgrounds. Old Faithful geyser is a big attraction, with a four-minute eruption every sixty-five minutes sending a column of steam and water 120 feet into the sky.

Leave Yellowstone by the Snake River south entrance, and follow U. S. 89 south for 336 miles to Salt Lake City. This takes you through wild Grand Teton National Park with its sharp-peaked mountains, lakes and glaciers. In the Mormon capital, see the Tabernacle and the Temple, and try a sink-proof swim in the lake at nearby Saltair.

It's 528 miles via U. S. 40 to Reno, Nevada, across the Great Salt Lake Desert. Near Wendover, on the Utah-Nevada line, you'll come to the concretelike surface of the Bonneville Salt Flats where many of the world's auto speed records have been set. The highway continues through the sage-covered hills and valleys of Northern Nevada's cattle country and southwest through sheep raising country to Reno.

After looking over the gambling casinos, drive the 139 miles to Sacramento via Virginia City, site of the Comstock Lode, one of the richest silver deposits ever discovered. Take U. S. 50 through

Garden of the Gods, near Colorado Springs,
is nature-carved cathedral of sandstone spires.
See National Park Vacation, page 12, and pages 50–51.

Carson City, then, along the eastern shore of brilliant blue Lake Tahoe, into Sacramento, California's capital and historic center of the Pony Express, with its relics of pioneer and gold-rush days.

U. S. 40 will lead you straight to San Francisco, eighty-nine miles away. But if you want to include Yosemite, turn south onto U. S. 99 to Merced, the Yosemite gateway. It's 187 miles from Sacramento to Yosemite through the rich San Joaquin Valley and the lofty Sierra Nevada Mountains. Yosemite is, of course, outstanding for its towering granite cliffs, famous waterfalls, and in summer, the nightly tradition of "The Firefall": a stream of embers poured from the edge of Glacier Point, 3254 feet into the valley. Thirty-five miles south of Yosemite Valley is the Mariposa Grove of Big Trees, one of the finest stands of giant sequoias outside Sequoia National Park, with many trees over 200 feet tall.

From Yosemite to San Francisco it's 257 miles via Merced and State highway 152 to Gilroy. From there you go north on U. S. 101 through San Jose, Palo Alto (where you might look into Stanford University's Memorial Chapel with its fine Italian mosaics), residential San Mateo, Burlingame and, as a climax, the Golden Gate.

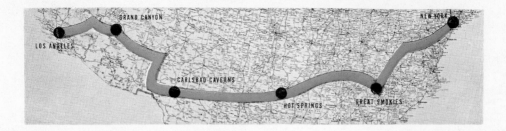

Coast-to-Coast: South

HAVING seen your country's northern wonders, here's a scenic way to take in the southern sector on your homeward trek. A leisurely, zigzag, 3800-mile route from Los Angeles to New York will show you the Grand Canyon, Carlsbad Caverns, the Great Smokies, the Blue Ridge and a bit of Mexico and other marvels in between.

Head out of Los Angeles on U. S. 66 through Pasadena and San Bernardino north to the Arrowhead Lake resort area. Here you have a breath-taking view of mountains, deserts, orchards and vineyards, before twisting down through Cajon Pass. Rolling desert leads through Victorville (scene of many a Western movie) and at Barstow you take U. S. 91 across the southern edge of the Mojave Desert to Las Vegas, Nevada.

Look over the glittering hotels, luxury motels, bars and gambling places that line "The Strip" and Fremont Street in this famous town. Then turn twenty-three miles southeast, on U. S. 93, to Boulder City, Hoover Dam, and lovely Lake Mead. Fish, sail or swim in the lake, and take a tour of the gigantic dam. It's 270 miles to Grand Canyon, via U. S. 93 to Kingman, U. S. 66 to Williams, and State highway 64 north to the Canyon's south rim. This multi-colored gash, from four to eighteen miles wide and 5700 feet deep, is one of earth's great wonders. Accommodations are good in Grand Canyon Village, center of South Rim activity, with the spacious El Tovar Hotel, Bright Angel Lodge and cabins, and a nearby auto cabin village. The South Rim Drives offer outstanding vantage points; conducted tours are available to all ma-

jor observation stations; and one- or two-day mule trips into the Canyon are conducted daily.

The 439 miles from Grand Canyon to Albuquerque are through magnificent desert country. Head east from the Canyon on 64, joining U. S. 89 south to Flagstaff, where you connect with U. S. 66, which skirts the Painted Desert and the Petrified Forest. To take in the entire Petrified Forest area, you can make a forty-one-mile detour out of Holbrook on U. S. 260, nineteen miles to the Forest's south entrance. Then you have a twenty-two-mile jaunt through a land of rainbow-hued fossil trees to rejoin U. S. 66 at the north entrance. Continue through the mountainous Indian country around Gallup to Albuquerque, the largest city in New Mexico.

From there, you turn south 272 miles to El Paso, Texas, through land rich in early Spanish and Indian associations. You follow the Rio Grande valley through which the Spaniards pushed up from Mexico, and towns along the way contain much early Spanish architecture. You'll pass through a town with the unbelievable name of Truth or Consequences, and perhaps visit nearby Elephant Butte Reservoir for some water sports.

El Paso is a big, bustling border city, and right across the Rio Grande lies Ciudad Juarez, your taste of old Mexico. You'll enjoy its pottery and other handicrafts, and there is also a bull ring.

Go east now 146 miles on U. S. 62–180 to Carlsbad Caverns, a fantasy of multicolored, sculptured limestone, perhaps the most beautiful caves in the world. Out of Carlsbad, it's 466 miles on U. S. 180 across rolling central Texas to Fort Worth, thirty-three miles more

to Dallas. In Fort Worth, look over Trinity Park and its adjoining Botanic Gardens; drive around and perhaps swim in Lake Worth. Dallas' Fair Park with its museums of fine arts and natural history are well worth visiting.

Leaving Dallas, you take U. S. 67 and State highway 7 some 311 miles to Hot Springs National Park on the southern edge of Arkansas' Ouachita Mountains. This is an area of wooded hills and valleys, with the medicinal spa of Hot Springs (its main street is lined with bathhouses) as its focal point.

U. S. 70, which will get you to Little Rock, capital of Arkansas, noted for its rose-covered residential areas, continues for 139 miles to the Mississippi and Memphis, Tennessee, a cosmopolitan cotton capital, hub of the river area between St. Louis and New Orleans. Dinner and dancing in a hotel roof garden overlooking the moonlit Mississippi have a special quality here.

It's 325 miles across Tennessee to Chattanooga on U. S. 64, through rolling country, across the southern end of huge Kentucky Lake, into the Cumberland Mountains. You pass through Sewanee, seat of the University of the South, with its 1000-acre campus, then you drop down the mountains to Chattanooga in its river valley. Go up to Chattanooga's Lookout Mountain for the view of the Moccasin Bend of the Tennessee River, and the stunning sight of mountains rolling in all directions. From Chattanooga to Knoxville you can take either U. S. 11 (the Sweetwater Valley route, 114 miles) or U. S. 27 and 70 (the Tennessee River route, 120 miles). The first carries you up a peaceful valley which is noted for its educational institutions, and the second gives you a chance to fish, boat or swim in

Bryce Canyon National Park, in Southern Utah, has fifty-six square miles of pink-hued fairy castles.

the great lake formed by the TVA Chickamauga Dam.

Knoxville is the western gateway to the Great Smoky Mountains, and the 127-mile route through Great Smoky Mountains National Park, via U. S. 441 and 19, brings you to Asheville, North Carolina. On the way, you'll climb into the high Smokies, up the crest of the mountains to Clingman's Dome for fabulous views of peaks, gorges and valleys. At Asheville, home town of novelist Thomas Wolfe, take in the Vanderbilts' Biltmore House, a superb French Renaissance château open to

the public, set in 12,000 acres of farm and forest. The grand spiral staircase is most spectacular.

Now hit the Blue Ridge Parkway, 391 spectacular miles winding through the Black Mountain Range and Pisgah National Forest, past 5939-foot Grandfather Mountain, across the high, rolling plateau of North Carolina, to its junction with Virginia's equally spectacular Skyline Drive at Rockfish Gap, near Waynesboro, Virginia. Go seventy-five miles up the Skyline Drive through Shenandoah National Park to Panorama, and there either turn off eastward

for Washington, D.C., or take the eighteen-mile round-trip run west to Luray for a look at the famous caverns. From Panorama, it is eighty-three miles to Washington through the fox-hunting and Thoroughbred-raising Piedmont.

In Washington, certainly you'll see the Capitol, the White House, the Washington Monument, Lincoln Memorial, and everything else there's time for. Then turn New Yorkward. The most direct route is the new expressway to Baltimore, U. S. 40 to the Delaware Memorial Bridge turnoff, and the New Jersey Turnpike to the Lincoln Tunnel.

Southwest Wilderness

SOME of the least known but most photogenic country in the United States may be explored in a thirteen-day Travelworld tour by chartered bus and Jeep, or much of it may be covered in your own car. As recently as 1946, much of the country traversed had never been seen by a white man. Running every two weeks from the middle of June to the end of September, the tour starts and ends at Albuquerque, New Mexico, and takes in Taos, Aspen, Colorado National Monument, Arches National Monument, Monument Valley, Navaho National Monument and Canyon de Chelly.

The first day you go on a tour of Albuquerque, Santa Fe and Taos, then out to Pueblo de Taos, an ancient, pre-Coronado Indian village of multi-tiered adobes, where traditional Pueblo dances are presented. You stay overnight at Taos.

The second day, you drive north along the Rio Grande, past peaks soaring 14,000 feet and more above sea level, and stop at Fort Garland, with its mementos of Kit Carson. The great peaks of the Sangre de Cristo Range come into camera view, and at Salida you ride to the summit of Monarch Pass (11,312 feet) and see narrow-gauge ore trains in operation.

The third day, you traverse one of America's most scenic mountain roads, north to Buena Vista at the foot of 14,399-foot Mount Harvard, then over 12,000-foot-high Independence Pass to Aspen, ski resort and summer cultural center. You'll want to photograph Maroon Lake and the Maroon Bells, three of Colorado's most photogenic peaks, then follow the tumultuous Roaring Fork River into Glenwood Springs, where you swim in a 600-foot-long pool fed by hot and cold sulphur springs.

On the fourth day, you follow the Colorado River through spectacular gorges to Grand Junction, Colorado, and at nearby Colorado National Monument you explore strange rock formations and tremendous canyons.

Next day at Cisco, Utah, you leave paved roads and enter the labyrinth of great canyons sculptured by the Colorado River. From Deadhorse Point you get a view rated by many as more spectacular than any of the Grand Canyon overlooks. The sixth day you spend at Arches National Monument, with its beautiful cobalt skies, twisted junipers, and giant, many-hued natural arches. The seventh day you head for Monument Valley through one of the least known sections of America, the Four Corners, where Colorado, Utah, New Mexico and Arizona meet. You see brilliantly colored desert ranges near Bluff, Utah, rock formations near Mexican Hat, and the Goosenecks of the San Juan River gorge. Then you arrive at Harry Goulding's Monument Valley Trading Post, and spend your eighth and ninth days exploring the sandy

Monument Valley, on Utah-Arizona border, has Navaho shepherdesses, desert obelisks.

wastelands in four-wheel-drive Jeeps, particularly the Valley of Mystery (first explored, by Harry Goulding, in 1946), with its prehistoric dwellings, weird rock formations and primitive Indian herdsmen.

On the tenth day you go south to the Indian trading post at Kayenta, and a Jeep takes you to Betatakin, a prehistoric cliff dwelling in the Navaho National Monument. On the eleventh day, you visit the mesa-top Hopi villages of Old Oraibi, Hotevilla and Mishongnovi, stopping for the night at Window Rock, headquarters of the Navaho Reservation. You Jeep it again on the twelfth day, into Canyon de Chelly, the historic natural fortress of the Navaho tribesmen. Sheltered by sheer canyon walls are more than 300 prehistoric ruins and the hogans of present-day herdsmen. Your last day, you ride back to Albuquerque via the mesa-top Indian village of Acoma.

National Park Vacation

ON a two-week, 2200-mile circle tour out of Denver by automobile, you can drive through this country's most impressive mountain scenery and visit four of the greatest National Parks: Rocky Mountain, Yellowstone, Grand Teton and Mesa Verde; two National Monuments: Arches and Black Canyon of the Gunnison; Cheyenne, Cody, Salt Lake City, Pikes Peak, the Garden of the Gods and Colorado Springs.

Head for Rocky Mountain National Park via U. S. 6 to take in the Denver mountain parks. From Golden, drive to the summit of Lookout Mountain to see Buffalo Bill's rock tomb and a panorama of snow-capped peaks. Cross the summit to U. S. 40 and, from Idaho Springs, take a short side trip on the Mount Evans scenic drive, highest auto road in North America, 14,260 feet above sea level, affording indescribable views.

Get back on U. S. 40, crossing the Continental Divide at 11,314-foot Berthoud Pass, then take U. S. 34 into the Grand Lake entrance of Rocky Moun-

tain National Park. You wind up the Rockies' western slope now, in one of the highest regions of the U. S., where even the valleys are 8000 feet above sea level and more than sixty-five peaks top 10,000 feet. You're heading for the Trail Ridge Road, which runs for four miles at 12,000-feet-plus. From its high point, 12,183 feet up, you look out onto the sheer walls and jagged snowy peaks of the rugged Front Range, the Never Summer Mountains, the Mummy Range; you peer dizzily down into river-threaded valleys thousands of feet below. The road drops steeply on the Rockies' eastern side and gives you breath-taking views, including Iceberg Lake and its floating ice blocks, glimpsed from atop a 350-foot cliff. Take the fork to Estes Park and stay overnight.

You'll want a day and another night there, to see Bear Lake and Moraine Park, explore around 14,255-foot Longs Peak (highest in the Park). Then, on your third day, move on via U. S. 34 and 87 to Cheyenne, Wyoming, where, if it's last week in July, you'll catch the Frontier Days celebration. Continue to Casper and stay overnight.

See sylvan Casper Mountain Park; then at Buffalo, turn west to the Big Horn Mountains, which rise abruptly out of the Great Plains, crossing them via U. S. 16 and the 9666-foot-high Powder River Pass. Stop at Cody, one of Wyoming's most scenic areas, where you'll want to see deep, narrow Shoshone Canyon and Buffalo Bill Dam. In July and August, you can catch the nightly Wild West show too.

Early on your fifth morning, you enter Yellowstone, oldest and largest National Park, by way of Yellowstone Lake, home of the once-almost-extinct trumpeter swan (the largest waterfowl in the U. S.), and the rare white pelican. Turn north on the park's loop road and stop at the Grand Canyon of the Yellowstone, one of *the* superlative sights of the continent. From Inspiration Point, jutting into the center of the 1000-foot-deep canyon, you look straight down on the foaming river, and to the southwest you see the great Lower Falls

taking a 308-foot plunge, twice that of Niagara's. The jagged walls of the canyon, predominantly yellow, are mottled with infinite colors. Get another stunning angle on Lower Falls from Artist Point, standing on a platform with 800 feet of air under you, and still another (down 400 steps!) right at the falls' brink. The walk to the brink of the 122-foot Upper Falls is rewarding, too, and much easier.

Drive on northward to Mammoth Hot Springs, detouring to the summit of 10,346-foot Mt. Washburn for a view across the park to the mountains of Montana and Idaho, and stopping to see the 132-foot Tower Falls. Stay overnight at Mammoth Hot Springs and, next day, explore the gigantic, vividly colored terraces built up by the springs. Drive slowly southward then to Old Faithful, taking the side roads, too, seeing magnificent geyser eruptions, colored pools, boiling springs. Some of the thousands of geysers go off every few years, others every few minutes. At Old Faithful stay overnight and spend the next day having your fill of its hourly shows and rushing to announced eruptions in nearby geyser basins.

Leave the park, on your eighth day, via West Thumb Junction, driving south on U. S. 89 to Grand Teton National Park, which contains the most Alpine of American mountains. This bunched-up range has spike-sharp peaks that shoot 3000 to 7000 feet straight up from Jackson Hole to altitudes over 13,000 feet. Stay overnight at Jackson Hole and spend next day exploring the park's lakes, glaciers and canyons on foot or horseback.

Continue via U. S. 89 through the canyon of Wyoming's Snake River, and via U. S. 91, past Great Salt Lake into Salt Lake City, at the foot of the Wasatch Mountains. Stop there overnight and take a day to see this hub of Mormonism and Utah, particularly the Tabernacle, Mormon Temple and State Capitol. Drive out to Saltair for a swim in the lake where you can't sink, the earth's saltiest body of water except the Dead Sea.

From Salt Lake City, if you have a few extra days, you can make a swing south, via U. S. 89 to Bryce, Zion and Grand Canyons, picking up this tour again at Mesa Verde. Otherwise, you, turn off U. S. 89 outside Provo, taking U. S. 50 to the junction with 160—a stretch that is mostly high, hot desert. About thirty-two miles down 160 a short side road takes you into Arches National Monument. Come back to 160 and drive on to Mesa Verde National Park and stay the night.

Spend your twelfth day seeing this amazing relic of prehistoric Indian civilizations. Located on a mesa rearing 2000 feet above the plain and gashed by deep canyons, the park contains dwellings dating from A.D. 1 to 1300. Cliff

Palace, the largest ruins, is a village of 200 rooms, twenty-three kivas, eight floor levels, all in one huge cave. Spruce Tree House, the best-preserved ruins, has 114 rooms in a single cave, with many original roofs intact. Fire Temple is an unusual ceremonial structure.

Go via Durango, past 14,000-foot peaks, to Montrose. Turn east on U. S. 50 and then take State 347 into the Black Canyon of the Gunnison National Monument, a stupendous spectacle. You lean over a fantastically hewn, knife-slit gorge to look down more than 2000 feet, feeling that, if you tried, you might touch the opposite rim, only 1300 feet away at the closest point. Below, the river channel narrows to a minimum forty feet.

Back on U. S. 50, you run through a green canyon, a fisherman's paradise, then climb over Monarch Pass. Just before Canon City, turn off to the Royal Gorge of the Arkansas River, 1100 feet deep, narrowing to a minimum of thirty feet at the bottom, and spanned by the world's highest suspension bridge. Take a ride on the steep Royal Gorge Railway. North on State 115 is Colorado Springs, where you stay overnight.

Spend your last day around Colorado Springs, taking in particularly the luxurious Broadmoor Hotel, The Garden of the Gods' vivid red sandstone spires and spines, and Pikes Peak. Climb the peak, either by the grueling auto road or the cog railway, for a suitably tremendous farewell view of the Rockies.

Tollgate Rock on Wyoming's Green River, near famous pioneer crossing, was named for Mormon tollgate.　　　13

*Burke Hollow, Vermont, is typical
of neat New England villages.*

Historical Northeast

ON a week-long 800-mile circle trip from New York City in your own car, you can recapture many of the stirring moments of the American Revolution, see some of the Northeast's most beautiful scenery, visit Lake George, Montreal and Tanglewood.

From New York head north over George Washington Bridge onto Route 9W, which parallels the Hudson as far as Albany, riding atop the sheer Palisades, remnant of a prehistoric volcano, for the first few miles. Five miles south of Nyack, detour a mile to Tappan, associated with the Benedict Arnold–Maj. John André tragedy, and see the De Wint Mansion, the Seventy-Six House and the hill where André was hanged.

Back on 9W, beyond Nyack, you can glimpse Sing Sing Prison across the river at Ossining. Stop at Stony Point Battlefield Reservation, stormed and captured by 1200 Continentals under Gen. "Mad Anthony" Wayne on July 6, 1770. Then, in Palisades Interstate Park, see the remains of Fort Clinton.

Just above Highland Falls, U. S. 9W becomes the hair-raising Storm King Highway, twisting 500 feet above the Hudson. Take a short detour to the U. S. Military Academy at West Point, see the cadets' precision marching, hike along Flirtation Walk, browse through the remains of Revolutionary forts. Get back onto 9W and go north to Newburgh, where you stop overnight. See the Hasbrouck House, Washington's headquarters in the last years of the Revolution.

Just above Highland you see FDR's Hyde Park estate and the Vanderbilt Mansion, both now National Historic Sites. Cross the Mid-Hudson toll bridge for a close-up look. Come back to 9W, and drive on to Kingston, which has overtones of the early Dutch as well as Revolutionary associations. North and west of Kingston you glimpse the Catskill Mountains, legendary home of Rip van Winkle.

At Albany, New York's capital, switch onto Route 4 to visit Saratoga National Historic Park and the Saratoga Battle Monument. The Battle of Saratoga, where Benedict Arnold helped defeat Burgoyne, was one of history's decisive battles. Buildings and fortifications have been restored as they were in 1777.

At Glens Falls, swing back to Route 9, then onto 9N to skim the western shores of Lakes George and Champlain. Lake George, cradled by high hills, has been called America's Lake Como. Stay overnight at the town of Lake George, and try to manage a dip.

Next day, drive to Ticonderoga, where, on the neck of land between Lake George and Lake Champlain, you visit old Fort Ticonderoga, restored as it was in 1775. Drive along Lake Champlain, with the glimmering waters and Green Mountains on your right, the rugged Adirondacks on your left. Make for Ausable Chasm where you explore jumbled rocks, caves and waterfalls.

At Champlain you enter Quebec Province, and immediately the road signs are in both English and French. Soon you're in Montreal, where you'll want to spend at least a day or two.

Return to New York City via Route 7 which parallels the eastern shore of Lake Champlain, cuts through Vermont's dairyland, skims the Green Mountains, then swings through the Berkshire Hills of Western Massachusetts and Connecticut. Stay overnight at Burlington, Vermont, on Lake Champlain. Take time here for a boat ride and climb the stone tower at Ethan Allen Park for a view that encompasses the Adirondack Mountains, the Winooski River and Green Mountains. Drop into Shelburne Museum, seven miles south of Burlington, for a glimpse of one-hundred-year-old buildings that recall America's past.

Next you're into one of Vermont's major winter-sports areas, with great sweeps of mountains cleared for skiers. You reach Bennington, a town steeped in Revolutionary history, then enter Massachusetts at Williamstown, in the heart of the Berkshires. Lenox and Stockbridge, set amid lovely wooded, rolling hills, are summer resorts, so stop overnight at either place. Both are only a few miles from Tanglewood, where the Boston Symphony Orchestra gives summer concerts.

You enter Connecticut at Canaan, next day, and, continuing through rolling hills and lovely old towns, hit the Merritt Parkway back to New York.

CALIFORNIA & HAWAII

CALIFORNIA
& HAWAII

Heading south from Monterey and Carmel,
State Highway No. 1 has the blue waters of the Pacific on one side and
the beautiful hills of the Santa Lucia Range on the other.

Another glimpse
of the Pacific shore
south of Carmel
shows the profusion
of wild flowers
that blanket the slopes.
The golden,
or California, poppy
is the State flower.

Giant redwoods
(*Sequoia sempervirens*)
form great belts of forest
north of San Francisco.
The "big trees"
(*Sequoia gigantea*)
stand in majesty
in isolated groves.

19

Emerald Bay is
forested cove on the
shores of Lake Tahoe,
whose 195 square miles
of blue waters are
partly in California,
partly in Nevada.
The lake's great depth
of 1600 feet
prevents freezing.

Worshiper kneels in the Temple of Kwan Yin in San Francisco's wondrous Chinatown, which is the largest Chinese settlement outside the Orient.

San Francisco is noted for its great hotels; the Palace Hotel with this superelegant
Garden Court dining room is one of the city's most historic.

23

Vineyards of Green Hungarian grapes cover the sides of Spring Mountain.
Beyond lies the Napa Valley and St. Helena, many of whose inhabitants are Swiss,
Germans and Italians from the vineyard sections of Europe.
Palm Springs (*on right-hand page*) is California's luxurious desert resort
for mid-winter sun seekers, at foot of the San Jacinto Mountains.

At Honolulu's famous Waikiki Beach (*left-hand page*), you hear the whoosh
of the surf moving in past Diamond Head where Pele, the fire goddess, once lived in the crater.
And you keep seeing the water turn turquoise and paler greens over the off-shore coral
and indigo blue in the depths. Waikiki is on Oahu, the island capital of the Hawaiian archipelago.
Above, you see some of the volcanic hills that break up the islands into tiny, lovely fragments.
Remote Waipio Valley (*above*) is an almost Polynesian pocket on the big island of Hawaii.

Diamond Head is one of the best-known travel landmarks in the world, its crater now green with growing things and its base ringed tight by the exotic metropolis of Honolulu.

THE NORTHWEST & ALASKA

THE NORTHWEST
& ALASKA

Mount St. Helens, with a hat of mist on its 9671-foot summit,
is reflected in Spirit Lake, in Southern Washington.

Mt. Hood, Oregon's highest peak, dominates brilliantly flowered Hood River Valley.

The 11,245-foot glacier-capped volcanic mountain is great center for skiing, climbing.

The 1200-mile-long Columbia River cuts great scenic swath through Cascade Mountair

far bank is Washington, in foreground Oregon, from Columbia River Highway.

Climbing 14,408-foot
Mount Rainier
is a two-day adventure
for the hardy.
Many climbers make
last lap at night to avoid
sun-softened snow.

From a glacier
on Mount Rainier's flank,
more than two miles up,
climbers see the Cascades
rolling southward
in mighty billows.
Mount St. Helens is at top right.
In top center of left-hand page
you see Mount Hood
100 miles away in Oregon.

37

At dusk, the crowded sky line of the great port of Seattle
is silhouetted against Mount Rainier, glowing pink in the sunset.

At Celilo Falls on the Columbia, fishermen net salmon from platforms.

Angler fights trout in swirling waters of Tye River, east of Seattle.

Sun Valley is Idaho's famous mile-high resort in the Sawtooth Mountains, with eight ski lifts and year-round recreational facilities. At right, Number 27 is set to take off in annual kids' race, figure-skating star does a ballet jump on all-year ice rink, and vacationers get ready for an old-fashioned sleigh-ride.

Pend Oreille Lake
is in the scenic wonderland
of Northern Idaho, and is
the state's largest lake.
Its beauty is matched
by the great sport it offers;
30-pound trout live here!

The Sawtooth Range reaches its streaked blue domes into the sky of South Central Idaho.

Juneau, capital of Alaska, has an overpowering natural setting, with massive mountains touching its back. It once served rough, tough gold prospectors; now every summer brings a new kind of rush, tourists in search of a stimulating, vigorous vacation.

The Ice Age still grips much of the coast of Alaska. This is Hubbard Glacier, near the village of Yakutat, shoving its beetling ice cliffs into Disenchantment Bay.

THE ROCKIES & PLAINS

THE ROCKIES
& PLAINS

Riders at Ghost Ranch, sixty-five miles northwest of Santa Fe, New Mexico, are on their way to sunset rendezvous at dramatic Chimney Rock.

The Teton Range
rules the sky line in
Grand Teton National Park,
Wyoming, just west
of the Continental Divide.
The peak at right
is 12,594-foot Mt. Moran,
with lovely
Jackson Lake below.

Garden of the Gods, Colorado's red-rock wonderland, is near Colorado Springs

n the background is Pikes Peak, most noted in state, though 27 others are higher.

Rolling uplands on western slope of Colorado's Rockies, near Cimarron, make excellent grazing grounds for shee

Bony peaks of San Juan Range, in Southwest Colorado, light up with brilliant colors at sundow

In such vast pastures, when strays are separated from the flock, the rancher searches for them in a chartered plane.

The range is a solid, sharp-spined wall of granite . . . one of the last, most spectacular frontiers in the Rockies.

Eight hundred years ago
the Colorado cliff dwellers
hewed out, stone by stone,
the first skyscraper
cities in America.
Cliff Palace, the largest
of these, was a busy village
of some 400 people,
with apartment-like homes
four stories high.

The red-roofed Broadmoor Hotel at
Colorado Springs was built by Spencer Penrose
to be "permanent and perfect."
The hotel comes close to fulfilling
its specifications in comfort and durability.
Since it opened, in 1918, there have been
many innovations, like water cycling
on the lake (*above*), and spectacular additions,
like the roofed-over rodeo grandstand
(across Broadmoor Lake from hotel, *right*).

Dark Cheyenne Mountain looms over the Broadmoor's acres

he Italian Renaissance hotel and its elaborate grounds are in lovely section of Colorado Springs.

Desert Inn is one of the palatial
resort hotels in Las Vegas, Nevada, noted
for sun by day, gambling by night.

Wide-open legal gambling flourishes in
Reno and Las Vegas and throughout Nevada.
This is the elaborate Golden Nugget,
Las Vegas spot that rivals Harold's Club in Reno.
Ten or more games of chance are offered,
plus bars, restaurant, floor shows.

Looking down, or looking up, the eye is stopped by splendid spectacles
all over Utah. *At left*, the 3000-foot-deep chasm of the Colorado is seen from lonely
Dead Horse Point. Above is the 10,500-foot-high ridge
of Mt. Olympus, part of Salt Lake City's guardian ring of mountains.

A little exertion on foot or horseback pays lavish
scenic dividends in Utah. Here is Zion Canyon from the East Rim Trail,
looking downward through the sheer-walled valley to the highway, 3000 feet below.
Through much of its course, the Canyon is about as deep as it is wide,
but in the Narrows, it comes down to less than 50 feet.

The strange Checkerboard Mesa displays a weirdly cracked expanse of stone
to tourists just inside the east entrance to Zion National Park, Utah.

Boisterous old times in the Dakotas come back to life when Deadwood throws its annual "Days of '76" celebration. *At right*, a simple memorial by a church on Pine Tree Indian Reservation, South Dakota, commemorates the last big clash between redmen and white.

At Mount Rushmore National Memorial, in the Black Hills of South Dakota, you see giant granite faces of George Washington, Thomas Jefferson, Theodore Roosevelt, Abraham Lincoln.

65

Kansas Free Fair, held every September at Topeka, offers thrill rides and midway attractions, harness racing, livestock judging.

THE SOUTHWEST

THE SOUTHWEST

From Maricopa Point, on the south rim of the Grand Canyon,
you get a spectacular view of the buttes and clefts.

The defense of the fortress of the Alamo, near San Antonio, Texas,
is one of the great episodes of American history.
It cost the lives of the entire garrison: Barret Travis,
the commander; Jim Bowie, designer of the bowie knife;
Davy Crockett and his Tennessee Boys; a total of 187 men.
Taken with a red filter, this glowing photograph
symbolizes a freedom won with blood.

At San Antonio's Fiesta San Jacinto, a happy reveler
holds a shiny *piñata* in his left hand.

Much Texas wealth comes from oil production
which has gone to more than one billion barrels a year.
That wealth is spent in such luxurious places as
the Shamrock Hotel with its 165-foot swimming pool.

The skyscrapers of booming Houston thrust up from oil-rich, cattle-rich, cotton-rich Texas plains.
Several of the closely grouped central buildings were erected to house the offices of oil companies.
Largest city of Texas, Houston is a major shipping center connected with the Gulf Coast
by the Houston Ship Channel. Within the city's borders are 73 square miles of land.

At Gray Horse, in the Pawhuska area of Oklahoma, Osage Indians do traditional war ceremonial. Dancers wear battle dress, but drummers don't bother with regalia.

The sky line of Tulsa, Oklahoma, built on a mound, seems suspended above the horizon.
In the foreground is one of the refineries that make Tulsa the "oil capital of the world."
It is the administrative and distribution center for the petroleum industry
of the mid-continent region, with the headquarters of many oil firms.

Oklahoma's bounteous yield of oil and grain required the construction, near Enid,
of the largest grain elevators and independently owned oil refinery in the world.

Cowboys at Wichita Mountains Wildlife Refuge, near Lawton, ride herd on buffalo.

An Osage brave, in a headdress of eagle feathers, deer tail and turkey beard, chats with girl dressed in type of Osage blanket that is worn to dances.

U.S. Highway 66, near Kingman, Arizona, shows spectacular scene

motorists along this famous trail. See page 9 for tour using this route.

Sunshine and horse country . . . these are
two blessings that nature supplies abundantly in Arizona.
Below, some of the members of the 206-family
Western Saddle Club hit one of the breath-taking trails.

The White House, spectacular Indian ruin in Canyon de Chelly,
is niched into the towering red-sandstone walls,
impregnable and almost inaccessible.
This National monument is in northeastern Arizona.

Taliesin West, Frank Lloyd Wright's bizarrely beautiful winter quarters,
blends into the desert landscape north of Phoenix, Arizona.

At left, the Grand Canyon
is pictured in all its rugged,
purple majesty by Ansel Adams.
217 miles long, 4 to 18 wide
and a mile deep, the Canyon
is one of the greatest lures
to American travelers.
At right, picnickers enjoy
chuck-wagon food in Papago Park,
between Phoenix and Tempe.

83

The Southwest's most popular winter spa is Tucson, Arizona, a busy industrial city in the middle of a desert. Temperamentally, however, it is a fun town where folks take time to play. The square dancing is going on at Old Tucson, a set from the film *Arizona*. The city is sheltered by mountains 5000 to 9000 feet high.

Tucson's bright sun and dry, mild and equable climate
attracts many winter visitors, who frolic by scenic hotel pools
like that of the Hacienda del Sol. When they get the ambition to explore,
there are ruined villages of the ancient Pueblos nearby.

Against the background of ancient adobe buildings, Pueblo Indian performs his people's Eagle Dance in a striking homemade costume, at Taos, New Mexico.

THE MIDWEST

THE MIDWEST

Memorial Stadium at Minneapolis, home base of Minnesota's
Golden Gophers, seats 50,000 of the nation's most rabid football fans,
who turn out even with the thermometer at six below.

Most cosmopolitan thoroughfare in the Midwest, a street of moods and aspects, Michigan Avenue
brings to mind many of the world's glamour capitals. What seems to be the sky line of New York
at dusk (*left-hand page*) is actually Chicago, looking south down Michigan
along a piece of the Magnificent Mile. Elsewhere on and near the Avenue, massed flowers
in Grant Park might be blooming in the Luxembourg Gardens; Riccardo's outdoor café
suggests a *trattoria* in Rome; Oak Street Beach wears the sunny look of Rio;
and an esplanade on the Chicago River carries a touch of Venice.

Students pore over campus bulletins at the University of Chicago,
one of the world's great universities, with 96 buildings and 110-acre campus in Chicago.
Differing in many ways from the conventional liberal-arts college, the University
translates the city's pioneering spirit into rugged academic independence.
Mammoth 450-million-volt synchrocyclotron (*right-hand page*) probes nature of universe.

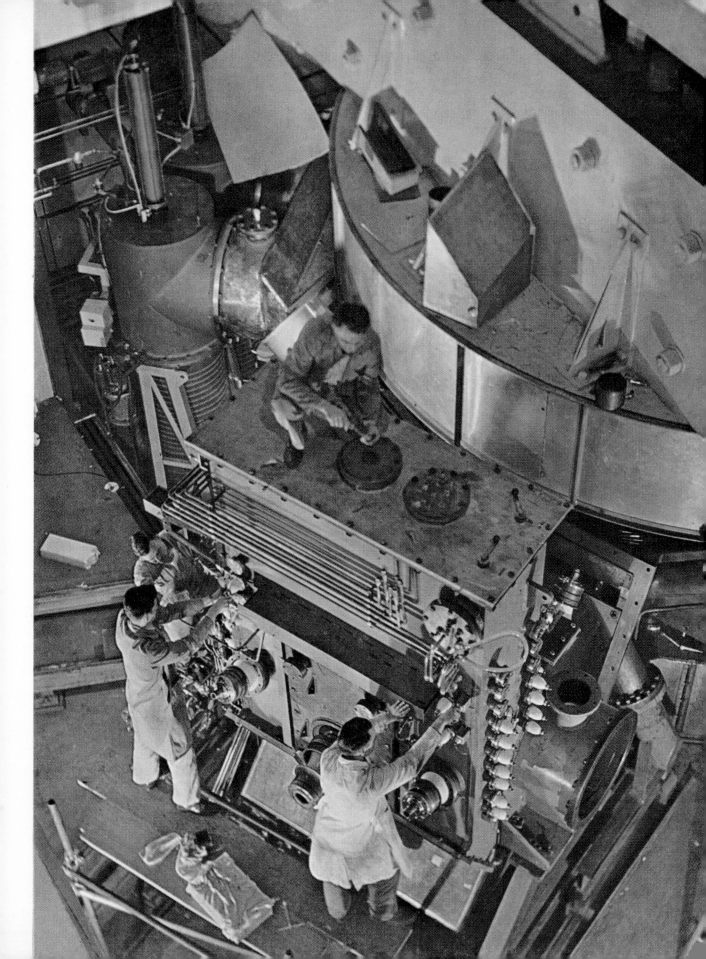

Commencement exercises
of Northwestern University
take place on the campus
at Evanston, Illinois,
with just-commissioned
ROTC officers in front rows.
Enrollment is nearly 20,000,
with 75-acre campus at Evanston,
14 acres in Chicago.

Part of resort atmosphere of Chicago's Edgewater Beach Hotel comes from $250,000 illuminated pool.

A big parade forms on the campus of Ohio State University, Columbus,
to advertise the annual military ball to student body of 18,500.

Split Rock Lighthouse (*left-hand page*) crowns a
beetling Minnesota cliff, warning mariners on Lake Superior
of the dangerous reefs at its foot. It is between Beaver Bay
and Two Harbors. A houseboat (*above*) needs no navigation
aids to wander lazily across Lake St. Croix, a
part of the St. Croix River which widens into a lake.

Minnesota's lake country (there are 10,000 lakes in the state) spreads out in a blue and green and primitive panorama beneath the wings of a Government seaplane.

NEW ENGLAND

NEW ENGLAND

New England's deep winter snows are followed by the bright days of summer
and an autumn decked with foliage of gloriously flaming brilliance.

A white lighthouse with a red hat marks the tip of Maine's Pemaquid Point, on one of the many rugged peninsulas that jut into the Atlantic Ocean north of Portland.

Weather vane at Prouts Neck Yacht Club symbolizes the seafaring coast of Maine.
Above is the restored and flourishing Country Store at Weston, Vermont.

New Hampshire's sharp-peaked Mt. Chocorua is often called "America's Matterhorn," and it is very likely the most photographed peak in the United States.

Dartmouth's three-day Winter Carnival, at Hanover, New Hampshire,
is a combined winter-sports meet, house party, and breathless college prom.

The Isabella Stewart Gardner Museum, popularly known in Boston as "Mrs. Jack Gardner's Venetian Palace," was imported stone by stone from Venice and other parts of Italy.

A swan boat sails serenely over the lagoon in Boston's Public Garden, adjacent to Boston Common.
Bridge is the world's smallest suspension bridge, a scaled-down replica of Brooklyn Bridge.

111

Boston, often called the Hub of the Universe, is clearly the true hub
of our national beginnings. The gold-domed State House,
built in 1795, towers over Boston Common where free speech
has always been a privilege. The Park Street Church, at Corner of Tremont,
was scene of first public singing of *America*.

Plymouth Rock has the date 1620
prominently carved upon it.
Historians may decry the landing myth,
but visitors revere the stepping-stone
and an iron fence is needed to protect it
from souvenir chippers. Guide in Pilgrim
costume tells hallowed legend.

Though today Plymouth is a thoroughly modern town, there are still
secluded spots and old homes that evoke its Pilgrim flavor.
The "Pilgrim" (*on right-hand page*) is resting between lectures
to tourists in a little park near Plymouth Rock.
Above, a costumed guide stands in the window of the
John Howland house, built originally in 1666 and restored in 1913.

Salem, Massachusetts, is a great historic treasure house. Cupolaed Custom House, flanked by lovely homes, looks as it did in old boom days.

Pioneers' Village, in Salem, is an accurate reproduction of typical units of a Puritan community about 1630. It was set up for Massachusetts' Tercentenary in 1930. It includes a replica of the *Arabella*, above, which brought Governor Winthrop and company to America. At top right is the monument to Salem's great literary figure, Nathaniel Hawthorne, at the head of Hawthorne Boulevard. Shown at right is the most celebrated spot in all historic Salem, the supposed setting of Hawthorne's novel *The House of the Seven Gables*.

The Wayside Inn, setting of Longfellow's famous *Tales*, is still in business near
Sudbury, Massachusetts, a suburb of Boston, as it has been since 1686.
Generations of wayfarers, including Washington and Lafayette, knew it as the Red Horse Tavern.

Old Sturbridge Village, in Massachusetts, brings back to life an 18*th* Century Puritan community and its ways. This is the Common, with 200-year-old red "saltbox."

A 20-foot water wheel still powers the Wright Grist Mill where grain is ground and sold. A blacksmith shop is another restoration of the old trades and crafts.

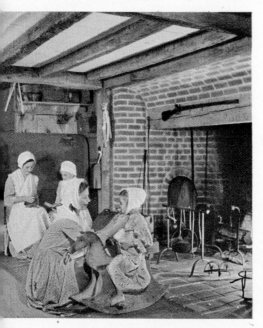

Authentic household gear in the kitchen includes an 18*th* Century rocking horse for baby. *At right*, Grant's general store, complete with post office and cracker barrel, specializes in nostalgic merchandise.

589
G. O & P. T. Co.
FINE TEAS
& COFFEE.
CROCKERY
SOLD AT
LOWEST PRICES.

119

Society names and tennis names make news at
Newport, Rhode Island, during August Tennis Week.
The grass courts of the Newport Casino, *top left*,
attract some of the world's best net stars.
The Providence Art Club, *left*, is on one of
the city's typically narrow, steep streets.
The red-brick Georgian house is representative
of the older architecture of Providence.

Roger Williams, founder of Providence, views his city from Prospect Terrace.
In center is white spire of First Baptist Meeting House, built in 1775.
The 26-story Industrial Trust Building dominates the sky line.

The Harkness
Memorial Tower
is regarded as
the landmark
of Yale,
at New Haven,
Connecticut.
White buckskin
shoes and
beer mug typify
the Yale scene.

122

THE CENTRAL NORTHEAST

THE CENTRAL
NORTHEAST

In the December dusk, a myriad lights glow in New York's spectacular sky line,
topped by the new television mast on the Empire State Building.

Over ten million
sight-seers have visited
Rockefeller Center
since it was built
twenty-one years ago.
Also known
as Radio City,
the group includes
the 70-story
RCA Building
and fourteen other
gray monoliths,
with their
230 elevators
and 16,500 windows.

126

Radio City Music Hall
is the world's largest
indoor theater,
seating 6200 people.
Its movies, orchestra and
stage shows,
with the great precision
dancing group, the Rockettes,
attract patrons from
near and far.
Above, the spires of
St. Patrick's Cathedral
rise in front of
the RCA Building.

Visitors to the glass-and-concrete headquarters of the United Nations average 2500 daily.
The total for 1954, ninth year after founding of the U.N., was 780,007 visitors.

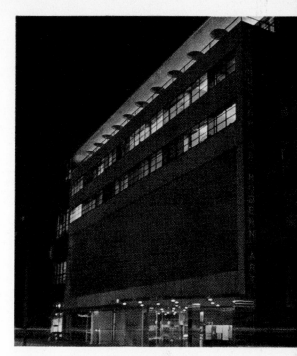

New York's Museum of Modern Art, opened in 1929, has an exciting, highly controversial collection, and holds outstanding exhibits such as Steichen's *Family of Man*.

New York's Metropolitan Museum, one of the world's finest citadels of art, occupies four city blocks along Fifth Avenue.

Television studios are important part of New York's entertainment headquarters.

131

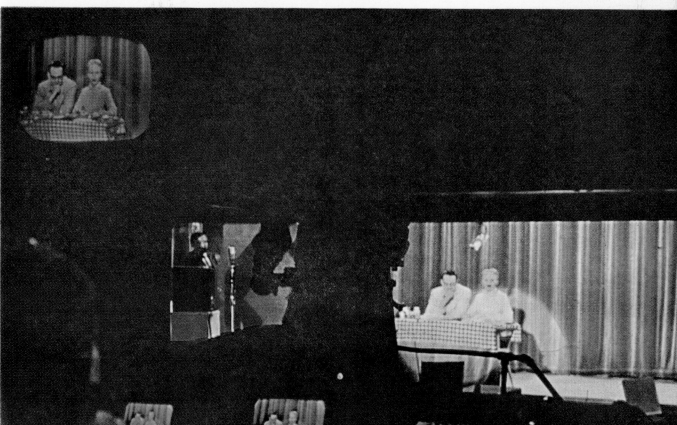

A throng attends Midnight Mass on Christmas Eve
at St. Patrick's Cathedral, seat of the Archdiocese of New York.

Tulip time brings crowds to the Botanical Garden, in seven-hundred-acre
Bronx Park, which also has the world-famous Bronx Zoo.

Once an almost inaccessible sand bar, Jones Beach on Long Island is now a great ocean beach, with many recreation facilities, parking for 15,000 cars. Water tower, top left, is landmark.

Cornell University, at Ithaca, bordering Cayuga Lake in the Finger Lakes District of New York, is one of the state's many great colleges. Clock Tower dominates the beautiful campus.

Southern New Jersey is famous for its tremendous stretch of white sandy beach,
extending from Sandy Hook, at New York's Lower Bay, 125 miles south to Cape May.
There are many deserted spots with wind-ruffled dunes and lonely loveliness,
and many like Atlantic City (*above*) with hordes of hotels and fun seekers.
Pine Valley Golf Club (*left-hand page*), in Southwestern New Jersey,
is considered one of the world's truly great courses—perhaps the toughest.

Delaware's Rehoboth Beach
looks out on the open Atlantic,
across a wide, clean strip of sand.
In the château country of Northern
Delaware there are many princely castles.
The air view at the right shows
Daybreak in the foreground, and
Oberod in the rolling land beyond.

138

America's past
is very much alive in
Ben Franklin's
Philadelphia.
Stately Independence Hall
(*left-hand page*) is the
home of the Liberty Bell
and of the Declaration
of Independence.
The Amish (*below*) and
the Mennonites (*right*)
are two gentle
and industrious
Pennsylvania
Dutch sects.

141

Gettysburg, Pennsylvania, was the scene of the three-day
battle that is generally regarded as the turning point of the Civil War.
Here, at Oak Ridge, the Confederates under General Lee
launched their vigorous attack on the Union forces under General Meade.
The Confederate cannon points toward the town.

Devil's Den made a perfect hiding place for a gray sharpshooter firing on Little Round Top.
The Trostle Barn, near the Peach Orchard, saw heavy fighting on second day of Gettysburg battle.
Shultz's Woods sheltered Confederate cannon placed by Lee's forces on the first day.

143

Now placid farm country, French Asylum at the bend of the Susquehanna near Towanda, Pennsylvania, once awaited Marie Antoinette, a Queen who never arrived.

From high on Bowman's Hill Tower, near historic Washington Crossing, the blue Delaware is seen winding past the autumn-tinted woods of Pennsylvania's Bucks County.

Valley Forge is a quiet encampment on a snowy day, with its black cannon and restored huts, but the thready notes of the Revolutionary trumpets still echo on the chill winds.

THE SOUTH

THE SOUTH

One of the most beautiful gardens in the world
is the wild and lovely Magnolia Gardens, near Charleston, South Carolina.
There are 25 acres of magnificent azaleas, camellias, magnolias.

149

Chesapeake Bay features midshipmen
and oyster-dredging craft.

Cut in two by
Chesapeake Bay,
the Maryland terrain has
great variety, with
rolling hills in the west
and this flat and
wild peninsula on the
Eastern Shore, seen
from the air near Easton.
The mansion is *Centaur*.

The Rose Room
at the White House
is assigned
to royal guests.

In the Family Dining Room, a crystal chandelier
bearing real candles hangs over the gleaming round table.

The New White House at Washington, completely rebuilt within the original
walls from 1950 to 1952, is the splendid home of America's highest office.
This view of the south front shows some of the beauty of
the seventeen acres of gardens, pools and fountains, lawns, trees.

Green Room of the White House features a fireplace of white Carrara marble and a Great Seal woven in the carpet. It is used by the President to entertain "informally."

The Blue Ridge Hunt, twenty-five strong, gathers for a hunt in front of the stunning façade of Carter Hall, near Berryville, one of Virginia's finest Valley estates.

Stratford Hall, on the lower Potomac
ninety miles from Washington,
is the ancestral home of the Lees of Virginia,
now restored to much of its early
grandeur by the Robert E. Lee Memorial
Foundation. The Great Hall, *at right*,
seems ready to welcome the evening's guests.

Monticello, *below*, was the beloved home
of Thomas Jefferson, author of the
Declaration of Independence, and founder
of the University of Virginia.
Never intending to make Monticello a
"show place," Jefferson spent sixty years
planning it to his own needs.

156

Governor's Palace

Bruton Parish Church

Wren Building, College of William and Mary

George Wythe House

Archibald Blair's Storehouse; King's Arms Barber Shop

Chowning's Tavern

These drawings by Mary Faulconer show twelve of the notable buildings of Williamsburg, Virginia's capital from 1699 to 1780, and now show place among Colonial restorations.

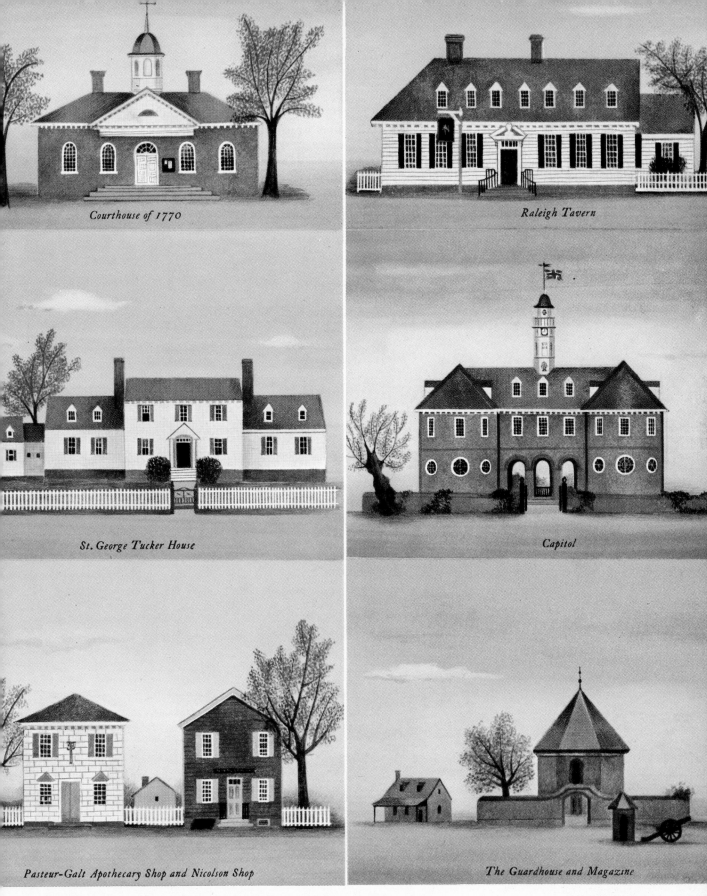

Courthouse of 1770

Raleigh Tavern

St. George Tucker House

Capitol

Pasteur-Galt Apothecary Shop and Nicolson Shop

The Guardhouse and Magazine

In this lively reincarnation of the busy Colonial capital, you feel vividly the essence of
the 18th Century city that helped produce the nation that the U.S. has become.

Cadets of the famed Virginia Military Institute, "West Point of the South," patrol over the Shenandoah Valley land which their Civil War ancestors contested so bitterly.

The pastoral West Virginia scene at top shows farmlands clinging to roller-coaster Alleghenies.
Below is an industrial stretch of the Kanawha River, at Marmet, with more billowing hills. 161

This is Missouri in the fall,
with broad farmlands
glowing in the afternoon sun.
The scene at left is a stretch of
rich Missouri River bottom land
just after the corn harvest.
Below is the Missouri River
town of Hermann,
settled by Germans in 1836.

163

Oak Alley, at Vacherie, Louisiana, was built in the 1830's by Jacques Télesphore Roma

s 28 columns match in number the double row of 90-foot oaks which form the handsome archway.

Louisiana's rivers and bayous were once lined with great plantations ranging from 500 to 1000 acres. Among those still existing are Parlange Plantation, *left-hand page*, occupied and operated by the same family since 1750.

Greenwood dates from the lavish 1830's. Its doors have silver hinges.

At Nottoway, a gardener thins out the encroaching Spanish moss.

Belle Grove, now in ruins, was one of the most fabulous of all plantation homes. It once played host to as many as fifty guests at a time, with their servants.

New Orleans goes wild during the Mardi Gras celebrations in the days before Lent.
Canal Street is jam-packed during parades. *At right*, a "King" and "Queen"
wait backstage at the Municipal Auditorium to make their royal entry.
Below, *right*, a "Lieutenant" marches with his "Maid."

In the Vieux Carré, New Orleans nights are long and gay.
You can hear all kinds of music, eat all kinds of food, drink all kinds of drink.
On left-hand page is the Quarter's world-famous restaurant:
You haven't dined until you have had dinner at Antoine's.

169

The sun sets over a Mississippi bayou, beyond Biloxi. Hundreds of these bayous are found along the Gulf Coast. They bear such varied names as Bayou Portage, where boat fishing for black bass

dfish and speckled sea trout is good, Bayou Acadian, Bayou DeLisle, and Rotten Bayou which affords
ood fishing for bass and bream. All are bordered by live oaks festooned with Spanish moss.

Twenty-two giant stone Corinthian columns are all that remains of the great five-storied mansion of Windsor, near Port Gibson, Mississippi. Built in 1861, it burned in 1890.

Under a king-size salvo of fireworks, the Royal Barge ties up beside the levee to open the
annual Cotton Carnival of Memphis, Tennessee. King and Queen then parade through city.   173

Magnolia-on-the-Ashley was once a great plantation. It lies about 20 minutes' drive from downtown Charleston. Its still-wild beauty makes it one of world's loveliest gardens.

Cypress Gardens, just north of Charleston on U.S. 52, offers azaleas, camellias, water lilies to visitors who travel by boat through cypress-marked avenues of inky-black waters.

Savannah, Georgia, has a hundred parks that dapple the city with green, many of them filled with luxuriant tropical plants—palmettos, oleanders, and bright azaleas. Monterey Square is one of many downtown parks.

FLORIDA

FLORIDA

At Miami Beach's elite Bath Club, midday dancing to the
accompaniment of a rumba band and a January sun is a delightful Florida custom.

Miami Beach from the air shows its spectacular row
of more than 350 luxury hotels, against the glistening
blue waters of the Atlantic. Biscayne Bay divides
the Beach from the City of Miami.
Below, the Jungle Gardens near Sarasota re-create
Florida's native subtropical forests.

Water sports at Cypress Gardens, on Lake Eloise,
hit a fast clip as girl athletes tear by the stands on water skis.
This show and the adjacent tropical gardens draw more than 700,000 visitors yearly.
Below, Bok Singing Tower near Lake Wales fills the air
with music from its 71-bell carillon.

184 The Fountain of Youth, at St. Augustine, harks back to Ponce de León's delusion, yearly drawing 300,000 tourists who try its water in hope or doubt or just for the heck of it.

In addition to Cypress Gardens (*pages 182-183*), Lake Eloise is the home of fighting game fish.
Not many years ago a wild swamp, the lake is just a few minutes' drive from Winter Haven. 185

Fort Lauderdale is a water-crossed yachting center, where all the best houses have a car in the front yard and a boat in the back. Seminole Village (*right-hand page*) is an active Indian community at Silver Springs. Caught between yesterday and today, a 97-year-old Seminole craftsman and his wife make dolls to sell to tourists.

Castillo de San Marcos, oldest existing
masonry fort in the U.S. (1672)
overlooks the entrance to St. Augustine harbor.

Okefenokee Swamp is a vast inundated region
of cypress, bay, and pine forests,
covering 660 square miles. One tenth of it is
in Florida, the balance in Georgia.
Much of this fascinating region is included
in the Okefenokee National Wildlife Refuge.

Opossum and baby find the swamp a haven;
so do raccoons, black bears, deer—and alligators.

Visitors to the Everglades National Park must stick to the few hard-surfaced roads, leaving the uncharted expanses of saw grass and palm to rangers and zoologists.

PHOTO CREDITS

INDEX

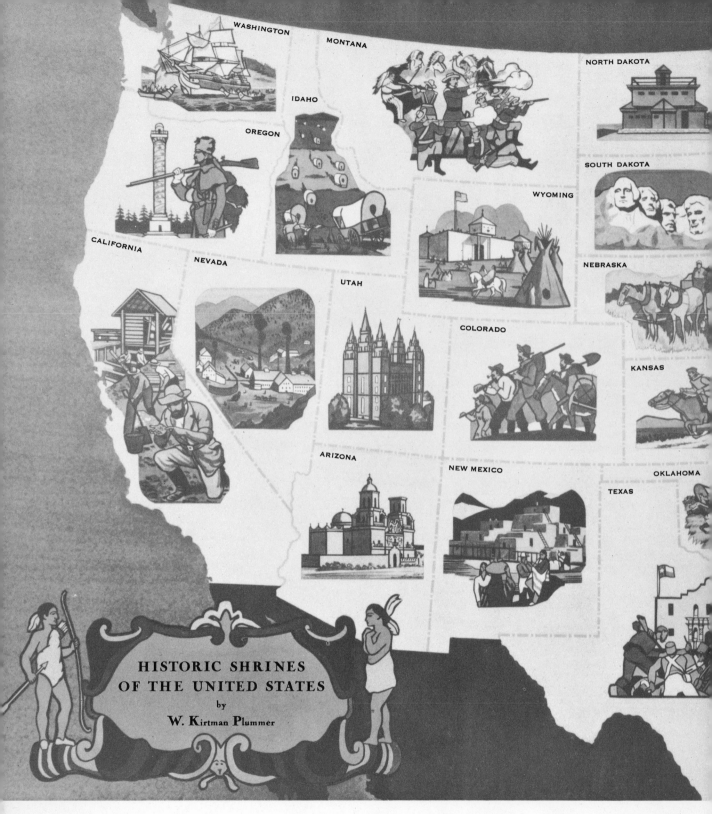

HISTORIC SHRINES
OF THE UNITED STATES
by
W. Kirtman Plummer

America's past lives in every one of the 48 states

Alabama. Battle of Mobile Bay, 1864.

Arizona. San Xavier Mission, Tucson.

Arkansas. Capitol buildings of Arkansas Territory, 1835; Little Rock.

California. Gold Rush; Sutter's Mill.

Colorado. "Pikes Peak or Bust," 1859.

Connecticut. Marine Museum, Mystic.

Delaware. Best-preserved 18th-Century town, New Castle.

Florida. St. Augustine, America's oldest city, 1565.

Georgia. Burning of Atlanta, 1864; cyclorama shows scenes of battle.

Idaho. Emigrant Rock on Oregon Trail.

Illinois. Lincoln Home, Springfield.

Indiana. Capitol buildings of Old Northwest Territory, Vincennes.

Iowa. Council Bluffs monument, eastern terminus of Union Pacific.

Kansas. Last Pony Express Station, Hanover.

Kentucky. Tomb of Daniel Boone, Frankfort.

Louisiana. Battle of New Orleans, 1815.

Maine. Fort Kent blockhouse.

Maryland. *Star-Spangled Banner* written at Fort McHenry, Baltimore.

Massachusetts. Plymouth Rock.

Michigan. Fort Mackinac, restored relic of French and Indian wars.

Minnesota. Snelling, farthest northwest Army fort till 1855.

Mississippi. Battle of Vicksburg, 1863.

Missouri. Dred Scott Courthouse.